CONTENTS

ILLUSTRATIONS

GENERAL ADVICE

To obtain the fullest enjoyment from rambling one must be properly dressed. Naturally footwear takes first priority. Boots must be worn on all rambles on the fells. These must be strong and waterproof, soled with either nails or "Commando" type rubbers as preferred. They should be worn over heavy socks, preferably two pairs.

Shorts should only be worn if a pair of light windproof overtrousers are carried. Also a spare pullover should be kept in your rucksac. Even in mid-summer the weather can change and become very cold on the higher fells.

Waterproof clothing is a very difficult thing to choose. Almost every anorack is not waterproof, but if it is absolutely waterproof you suffer from condensation. So it is better to concentrate on something windproof to wear and carry a plastic or proofed nylon anorack (which is very light) to put on over it in a really heavy downpour. But in wet weather in the Lake District on a ramble you will get wet eventually whatever you wear.

Next in your equipment must be a rucksac. There are many types on the market both with or without frames. The main point to remember is to get one sufficiently large to carry all you need comfortably, and that the load should be carried high on the shoulders, so a wedge-shaped rucksac with the thick end of the wedge uppermost is to be recommended.

You should always carry a one-inch to the mile map of the area you are walking in, a compass and a whistle and torch. You should be proficient in the use of the compass. The distress signal is six blasts on the whistle every minute.

Finally, to be fully equipped one must also carry a First Aid Kit and a few spare clothes.

Route descriptions of rivers and roads are left or right as facing the way you are going.

Times given are only approximate and in bad weather may take longer. Allowance for this must be made in your planning for the walk.

BUTTERMERE

The Buttermere Valley is the only Cumberland valley to possess three lakes—Buttermere, Crummock and Loweswater. Buttermere and Crummock are separated by a strip of low-lying land just over half a mile wide, but after very heavy and prolonged rain, these two lakes become one. Undoubtedly in the distant past, they were one lake. Most of the area is National Trust property.

Buttermere is a very charming lake, $1\frac{1}{4}$ miles long and half a mile wide, and is rather shallow, especially at the lower end, and nowhere is it more than one hundred feet deep. It is set deep in a basin of mountains which descend almost sheer into the lake on two sides, and the fells are well wooded with Scotch fir and larch, while at the head stands the noble fell of FleetwithPike.

Crummock is much larger than either of its two neighbours, being $3\frac{1}{2}$ miles long by three-quarters of a mile wide. Its most imposing features are Melbreak to the west and Rannerdale Knott, which juts out into the lake on the eastern or road side. There is a footpath round the Melbreak side of the lake, and a main road runs along the greater part of the eastern side. Behind Rannerdale Knott stands Grasmoor, mostly crag and scree on the Crummock side, but easy to climb from either Buttermere village or by Gaskell Gill.

The village of Buttermere stands between the two lakes, and consists of a church, school, two good hotels a Youth Hostel and a number of farms, the majority of which accommodate visitors.

Two miles from the village is Scale Force, the highest waterfall in England with a drop of 120 feet. It is perhaps not as pretty as other Lakeland falls, but its setting is unusual, as it is deep in a big ravine abounding with copse and fern. In wet weather, when the stream is in flood, it is often impossible to approach near to it.

Loweswater is about the same size as Buttermere, but is more than one hundred feet higher than Crummock into which lake it empties by a fairly large stream. It is even shallower than Buttermere, but equally as pretty.

Buttermere and Haystacks

Most of its shore is well wooded. The main road runs the full length of its northern shore while a rough cart track goes through Holme Woods on its southern shore. The best view is from the head of the lake with Melbreak prominent in the background.

The village of Loweswater possesses a church, post office and inn midway between the two lakes, and a number of scattered farms, several of them providing accommodation.

The three lakes are emptied by the River Cocker, which flows from Crummock through Scale Woods, down the Vale of Lorton to join the River Derwent at Cockermouth, a small clean and healthy market town dating back to 1215, when William de Fortibus was restored to his Manor of Cockermouth.

Cockermouth is an interesting town, surrounded by valleys, plains and mountains, all of which are easily reached by car or on foot. It is chiefly an agricultural centre, and is an important market town for dairy produce, cattle and sheep; the market on Mondays is a big affair. It has a public park containing tennis courts, bowling greens and amusements for the children. Situated on a hill directly above the town, the park gives a commanding view of the district that is difficult to surpass.

Cockermouth is the birthplace of the famous Lakeland poet, William Wordsworth, whose parents came to reside here in 1766. His house stands in the main street and is now National Trust Property, and open to the public.

Another attraction is the castle, standing like a sentinel at the entrance to the town from the Keswick side. It was built from the square-hewn stones of the Roman "Oppidum," but there are no authentic records of the town until after the Norman Conquest. In 1648, the castle was besieged by the Royalists, and the castle and its defenders suffered woefully before relief came on 29th September. The castle is open to visitors every day and is interesting for its unique dungeons, the Mild Kirk, and shields bearing the arms of former owners of the castle—Lucies, Percies, Nevilles, Umfravilles, and Multons. A wonderful view of the River Derwent and the surrounding country is obtained from the terrace.

Four miles up the Vale of Lorton is the charming old world village of Lorton, which is divided into two parts, High Lorton and Low Lorton, with the parish church in between.

High Lorton lies at the foot of Whinlatter Pass, which is the main road over to Keswick. About a mile-and-a-half up the pass is a stone bridge over a mountain stream. It is worth while leaving the road at this point and proceeding up the stream for half a mile as far as Spout Force, a really fine waterfall of about fifty-feet drop which is almost unknown to visitors. An unusual outcrop of rock in front of the fall enables the visitor to get a very close-up view. If desired the walk can be continued through the gap between Broom and Kirk Fells, descending Wythop Moss back to Embleton.

Two miles up the valley from Lorton the main road divides, the left-hand branch leading to Buttermere, and the right to Scale Hill and Loweswater.

Buttermere has a distinct place in our history, a place gained during the Norman Conquest. Unlike the rest of Britain, Buttermere was never subjugated, despite all that the Normans attempted. The rout of a great army ended the Norman efforts to bring the last remaining English stronghold to subjection.

In the years following the Norman Conquest of 1066, the English were driven farther and farther north by the Normans until the Lake District became their last stronghold, with Buttermere their secret headquarters.

For many years the refugees waged a guerilla warfare on the invaders, who were at a great disadvantage in the strange mountainous country, and consequently several Norman armies were lost in the various battles which took place. Determined to put an end to this resistance, Henry I gave orders that these "rebels" should be exterminated.

The English, led by Earl Boethar, were traced to their headquarters at Buttermere. The Normans, under Ranulf Meschin, established a camp at Papcastle, near Cockermouth, and regiments were withdrawn from Carlisle, Kendal and all the castles of the Eden valleys. These, with the addition of new troops recruited in Norway, made an overwhelming army.

After great preparations the huge army set out up the Vale of Lorton, full of confidences. A clever ruse by the English had been to divert the road at Rannerdale Knott so that the raiders would proceed up this road, which led to a very narrow valley. In this valley they concealed pits filled with stakes, and every contrivance and snare for killing men and horses.

After camping at Lorton for two days the great army moved forward. Afraid that the Rannerdale defences may not be strong enough to hold this huge army, defences were rapidly erected at Brackenthwaite, and here Boethar gave fight. In the struggle the losses on both side were enormous, but the Normans proved superior and the English slowly retreated, according to plan, to their Rannerdale defences.

As they retreated, they drew the advancing Normans up the fake road, where the main force of the English army lay hidden. At last most of the Norman army was well within the valley of Rannerdale, and Boethar, who was watching and directing the battle from a vantage point on Rannerdale, gave the signal. From all sides thousands of well-armed men, led by Earl Ackin, brother to Boethar, swept down on the invaders. The Normans were astounded, and terror and chaos were rife when Ranulf realising the dangers, gave the order to retreat. When the Norman formations got hopelessly confused and the routes of escape were blocked, a great crowd of berserkers rushed down the mountain-sides to where the confusion was greatest. There they slipped in between the horses, which they disembowelled as they passed beneath them. Sheer panic seized the invaders as thousands of them were slain, and what was once a proud army became a fleeing rabble. The Normans who managed to get out of the valley fled thankfully back to Lorton and Cockermouth.

Naturally the English suffered great losses too, and their battle leader, the Earl Ackin, was killed. He was buried on the present site of Buttermere Church, but later, in accordance with his wish, his remains were carried to the scene of the battle in the valley, and the hill was named Ackin's Howe.

Buttermere's place in history was assured by the last attempt of the Normans to capture this spot, an attempt which failed dismally, and left this corner of England free from the Norman yoke.

LAMPLUGH—BLAKE FELL

Between the two valleys of Loweswater and Ennerdale lies some interesting fell country providing several good walks. Here is one from Lamplugh.

At the bus terminus at Lamplugh Cross Inn the main road forks, the left fork being the main road to Cockermouth; the right is a secondary road, over which heavy traffic is prohibited, and goes by Lamplugh Church to Loweswater. It is along this second road that our walk commences.

About twenty yards past the inn right turn along a country lane which passes a farmhouse and leads into some fields. The path through the field is at first a wide cart track, but after passing through a gate becomes a mere footpath leading to a stile and stream. Continue through another field by a rough cart track passing through a farmyard at the top, Fell Dyke.

Cross the road and follow a lane, which starts on the other side, for about thirty yards, turning through the second gate on the right into a field.

A rough cart track leads from the gate up the field and through another gate, when it becomes a fenced track leading right into the fells. Soon a charming tree-planted ravine down which flows a small stream, appears on the left.

Shortly after you will reach Cogra Moss Reservoir, which supplies water to Frizington. The track runs alongside the full length of the reservoir at the foot of Knock Murton, which is the prominent hill on your right and well worth climbing. It is very steep but not so high, and half an hour will take the average climber to the top, from which is an extensive view of Ennerdale and the Ehen valley. The best approach is up the side facing Lamplugh, so commence climbing from the second gate on the Cogra Moss route after leaving Fell Dyke.

Those who take the bottom track will find themselves in a cul-de-sac at the head of the reservoir. A footpath rises sharply up the side of Knock Murton, rough in parts and bordered all the way by thick bracken and heather. Bilberries grow in profusion here in July.

At the top of the rise, the path joins the Forestry Road which goes round the side of Blake Fell. Across this road, the route lies up the hillside by the side of a wire fence which goes up the side of Middle Fell.

There is no distinct footpath, but the fence is sufficient guide as it will lead you right to the top of Blake Fell, which is the fell with the scree on its side coming down to the reservoir on the opposite side to Knock Murton. It is a long, steady climb, grass all the way, taking about forty-five minutes from the bottom of Middle Fell to the top of Blake.

The view from Blake Fell is very extensive, with a greater portion of the Solway in view, backed by the

Scottish hills. To the south lies Ennerdale lake, and to the east is a corner of Crummock, with Buttermere behind. Overlooking Crummock is the mighty scree side of Grasmoor. Melbreak hides a large portion of Crummock.

The descent is started in a direct line for Melbreak and Crummock Water, almost due east. There is no track, but the route is fairly easy. After proceeding for about one hundred yards swing left to drop down a grassy tongue formed between Carling Knott and Gravel Fell. High Nook Beck flows on the right of it. There are traces of a zigzag footpath down the tongue, but a sheep fold at the bottom near where a track crosses High Nook Beck is the best guide, so make this your objective.

On reaching the bottom, a track starting from across the beck may be followed, and this will lead to the main road between Crummock and Loweswater. For the purpose of this walk, however, do not cross the beck, but instead, follow a footpath which keeps to the left side for some distance, and then rises round the bottom of Carling Knott with a stone wall on the right. Soon, on the other side of the wall a thick plantation appears, and below is Loweswater.

The footpath continues to follow the side of the wall until it reaches and crosses a stream, Holme Beck. There is a good wide grassy track from here known as the Terrace, and the views down into Loweswater and across to Buttermere are really beautiful, and extend for quite a distance.

Passing through the next gate, the track swings to the right and follows a stone wall for about half a mile, eventually passing through a gate on to the main road. Turn left and follow this back to Lamplugh Church. The church, with its old lych gate is well worth viewing.

From the church, the road leads back to Lamplugh Cross, thus completing the circle.

Distance, 11 miles. Time in minutes :—Lamplugh Cross to Cogra Moss Reservoir, 25; Middle Fell summit, 45; Blake Fell, 20; High Nook Beck (sheep fold), 25; Holme Beck, 25; join road, 30; Lamplugh Church, 30; Lamplugh Cross, 15.

COCKERMOUTH—LOW FELL—LOWESWATER

Cockermouth is the starting-point of several good walks, and the next two are attractive, but not strenuous ones.

The first follows the main road from Cockermouth past the station in the direction of Egremont. About a mile from the town a lane on the left leads to Waterloo farm, passing the buildings on the right. Down another short lane the route crosses a small stream by a foot-bridge to enter a field. Pass up the centre of the field by a footpath to a stile at the top. The track continues across a second field and joins a road at the opposite end.

Turn left down this road and keep right at the first junction. Although a tarmac road it is narrow, and has interesting hedges on either side. At the bottom of a hill it crosses a beck and is joined by another similar road on the right, just before reaching Rogerscale. After crossing the second stream, pass through the first gate on the right and go up through a field to a farm, passing it with the buildings on your right. A well-defined track ascends the fell side above the farm, fairly steep at first and over-grown with gorse in parts, until it passes through a gate then becomes almost level through the next field to join the Whinfell Road.

Turn right along this road with a grass verge on either side. There is a good view on the right towards Cockermouth, and most of the route along which you have just passed can be seen.

Just over five minutes good walking along this road a grassy lane will be observed on the left and along which the route lies. There may be a little bog at the beginning in wet weather, but it soon reaches dry ground again, and the track is well defined for the next mile.

After about a mile the remains of a building is passed on the right. This is a sign to leave the main track and bear right at an agle of about thirty degrees up the field. At the top is a grand view of Crummock Water. In front, a little to the right of Crummock, a track will be observed on the nearest fell, zigzagging from a beck in the bottom up the fell side to the top. The top of this track is the next objective, and the best way to reach it is

From Robinson

to cross the stone wall on the right and walk round the fell side at roughly the same level all the way. It is rather like walking round the inside of a huge basin until you finally reach the top of the zigzag path on Sourfoot Fell.

At the highest point of this path is an iron gate. Pass through and then turn sharp left and walk to the end of the fell, about fifty yards on to a small hillock, Watching Point, from where is one of the finest views of Crummock and Buttermere available. The upper Lorton Valley lies almost underneath, while across is Grasmoor. To the right of Crummock is Melbreak, with Mosedale on the right. Red Pike and Great Gable lie directly behind Crummock.

Returning to the track, pass through the remains of an iron gateway, then bear right on to Darling Fell, descending from here towards Loweswater, joining the

Mosser Fell road lower down. Turn right along this road until it drops down to the hamlet of Mosser, with its small church standing isolated on a hillside about half a mile from the nearest house.

There are several road junctions, but they are well signposted. Our road joins one from Mockerkin, passes through a gate, then bears sharp left at the farms. Take the next right-hand fork 200 yards beyond the farms, and follow this for about a quarter-of-a-mile, where another lane branches off on the right to Akebank Mill. Follow this road for about one-and-a-half miles until it joins at right angles another secondary main road. Turn right down this road, then through the first gate on the left, and across the fields to Waterloo Farm. You have now completed the circle, and the first part of the ramble to Waterloo is retraced back to Cockermouth.

Distance, 16 miles. Time in minutes :—Cockermouth to Waterloo, 30; Whinfell Road, 65; Sourfoot (Watching Point), 75; Mosser Road 40; Mosser, 60; Cockermouth, 75.

COCKERMOUTH—VALE OF LORTON—LOWESWATER

This second walk from Cockermouth is up the Vale of Lorton by the Fisherman's track, following the River Cocker all the way from Cockermouth to Lorton.

The track starts at the railway bridge over the River Cocker just outside Cockermouth Station. It is best reached by walking along the line from the station, otherwise one must cross the railway from the Lorton road and then over the fields to the river. Keep the river on your right as you walk up it.

From the bridge this Fisherman's path is easy to follow, for it keeps close to the river as far as the first building at Southwaite. Here it crosses the road and continues up the lane to Lowfield, the next farm. Pass through the gate just before reaching the buildings, cross the field to the river, cross the fence by a stile, and continue up the river for another mile until a small square building, standing about fifty yards from the river, is reached. This is known as Stanger Spa, and it contains a six-feet-deep well of medicated water, good for skin diseases and rheumatism, either as a lotion or medicine. It has now fallen into disuse.

Continuing up the bank, Rogerscale is observed on the opposite side of the river, which then sweeps sharply to the left, then right again. At this second bend, leave the river and proceed across the field to a lane about one hundred yards away; this will lead to the village at Low Lorton.

Follow the road through the village, then turn right at the first junction to Low Lorton Bridge. Over the bridge, take the left fork and follow the road one-and-a-quarter miles to the houses at Thackthwaite. Just past the last house on the right, a lane commences up towards Smithy Fell, but as a stream flows down the lane in wet weather it may be advisable to walk up the field on the left until it reaches a pony track at the head of the lane. Turn right along this track which rises gradually, swings to the left, and goes almost due west. A litle farther on, it rises sharply by a series of zigzag bends to the summit of Sourfoot Fell. This is the path referred to in the last walk, and the rest of the route is as described in returning to Cockermouth.

There is an alternate route from Mosser Fell Road which is much longer, but in summer has the advantage that a bus might be caught back to Cockermouth. Instead of turning right to Mosser, turn left to Kirkstile, and follow the main road to Scale Hill. After crossing the river, the road rises sharply to Scale Hill Hotel, the Buttermere road joins it half a mile beyond where it may be possible to catch a bus back to Cockermouth.

There is also an occasional bus between Cockermouth and Loweswater village, enquiries should be made about times from the Cumberland Motor Services Ltd.

Distance :—Cockermouth to Sourfoot Fell, 8 miles; Sourfoot Fell to Cockermouth via Mosser, 9 miles. Time in minutes:—Cockermouth to Southwaite Farm, 65; Stanger Spa, 40; Low Lorton, 35; Thackthwaite, 35, Watching Crag, 50.

Grasmoor and Loweswater

GRASMOOR

The start of this climb is Lanthwaite Green, which lies alongside the road from Buttermere to Lorton at the top of the hill where the road leaves the lake. The track starts opposite the farm and crosses a small stretch of lowland to the foot of the narrow gap between Grasmoor and Whiteside.

The stream which flows down this gap, Gaskell Gill, is crossed and the track then rises sharply round the end of the scree of Whiteside, continuing up a very narrow ravine. The path is rough and narrow, but easy to follow as it keeps the beck on your right all the way to the summit.

The summit of the Coledale Pass is reached at the hollow between Hobcarton and Grasmoor. The route to Grasmoor starts short of the summit and bears right up the side of a stream. The summit of Grasmoor lies on the right of the course of the stream, and the climb is steep, but short, so that the summit can be reached in about half an hour.

Grasmoor—often incorrectly spelled Grassmoor—has the origin of its name in grise, meaning wild boar, so that it was probably the moor of the wild boar. It is fairly flat on the top, and to obtain a really good view, one must proceed west a few yards in the direction of Crummock to see over the side. There are three cairns, each giving a good view. Across Crummock and Buttermere is the Red Pike ridge with Gable prominent at the far end, and behind this is Pillar and Scafell.

Descend by walking due east along the plateau at first, then swing south in the direction of Robinson. There is no definite track at first, but one soon makes its appearance, and this leads down to the top of the Wandope ridge.

The descent now follows the narrow ridge down Wandope. The track is very distinct and easy to follow, and the views over Buttermere are very beautiful. The track continues down a long spur on Whiteless Pike, then the ridge broadens out as Blake Rigg is crossed, and an easy walk along the bottom soon leads back to Buttermere.

Distance from Lanthwaite Green over Grasmoor to Buttermere, 7 miles. Time in minutes:—Lanthwaite Green to top of Coledale Pass, 90; Grasmoor, 30; Buttermere, 70.

RED PIKE—HAYSTACKS

This walk commences at Buttermere Village. Pass to the left of the Fish Hotel and follow a cart track which passes down through two fields at the foot of Buttermere Lake and then crosses the river at the point just where it leaves the lake. The white-looking beck, Sour Milk Gill, which falls almost perpendicularly down the mountain-side, is a good guide. Cross this beck, and almost immediately a footpath commences to rise and wind through the thick plantation.

On leaving the wood the track continues to wind up the fell side until Bleaberry Tarn is reached. This small sheet of water lies at the foot of red scree which gives Red Pike its name. To reach the summit, the route goes to the right round the edge of the saucer in which the tarn lies, and although it is a fairly steep scramble the distance is short, and very soon the cairn marking the summit of Red Pike is reached.

The view can compare favourably with any other Lakeland fell, and it is one of the few spots from which five lakes can be seen at once. Almost underneath lies Buttermere, and one feels as if one could throw a stone into it. On a calm day the barking of dogs and various other sounds can be plainly heard coming from the valley. Farther to the west lies Crummock and Loweswater, the former broken in parts by Melbreak. Away behind Buttermere through the Newlands Valley, to Derwentwater, with all its islands. To the south - west, almost all of Ennerdale Lake can be seen. The mountain aspect is also very grand, Steeple and Pillar appearing very close.

To the east around some crags is another peak, which is the next objective in this ridge walk, and in a few minutes the summit of High Stile is reached. Although its 2,643 feet is 164 feet above Red Pike, the view is nothing like as extensive, although Pillar appears nearer. On the Buttermere side are some dangerous crags, and care must be taken to avoid them. A footpath leads from High Stile along the ridge towards High Crag.

From the cairn on High Crag descend to the left, following the direction of a wire fence. It is quite steep and rough until it reaches Scarf Gap Pass. If it is desired to shorten the route, follow the pass back to Buttermere.

For an easier walk, start at Buttermere, and walk along the High Stile side of the lake until the track which comes from Gatesgarth is reached at the head of the lake. This is Scarth Gap Pass which rises sharply for the first hundred yards, after which it climbs gradually to the top.

The route up Haystacks starts from the cairn marking the summit of the pass. Looking up above the crags can be seen a rock on which is a long stake marking the summit of Haystacks, and this is your next objective.

At a glance the crags appear rather forbidding, but a path which commences from the cairn on the top of Scarf Gap begins to wind up and round these crags, and actually it turns out to be quite an easy scramble, and the top should be reached in less than half an hour.

Haystacks consists of a rather large top on which are numerous small peaks—rather like a lot of haystacks —and on several is a stake placed by the Ordnance Survey. Between some of these are small mountain pools, the largest of which is Innominate Tarn, containing several small rocks like islands. The whole resembles a miniature Lake District, and some time can be spent on the summit passing from peak to peak.

The very fine views include three lakes, Buttermere, Crummock and Ennerdale; Pillar with its famous rock lies across the Liza Valley, while Gt. Gable lying directly directly behind Innominate Tarn makes a very impressive picture. To the north is Fleetwith Pike, which is backed by Robinson and Dale Head.

The path begins to descend and passes to the left of Innominate Tarn, and shortly after crosses the top of a very deep gully which drops towards Buttermere lake. Then it winds round to the right below more crags and comes to Black Beck Tarn.

Passing the bottom end of the tarn, the path crosses some open country to the right of two small hills, winding round the second to the left until it strikes a well-marked footpath coming off Brandreth, almost opposite the Honister quarries on Fleetwith.

The path now passes below Green Crag, then crosses the beck on the right to join the pony track from the quarries which leads down Warnscale Bottom to link up with the Honister Pass road at Gatesgarth.

A longer, but splendid, alternative route from the union with the Brandreth track on Green Crag is to cross the beck in a line for the quarries observed on the fell opposite. Climb a short way up Fleetwith, but not as far as the quarries, then bear left and make for the summit ridge. The ground is grassy but uneven, and there is no footpath, but half an hour of easy climbing should lead to the summit ridge. Bear left along here to the cairn marking the summit of Fleetwith Pike.

The view is very extensive; the crags on Haystacks can be closely examined, whilst Gable, Glaramara, the Helvellyn range, and the Dale Head group are all in sight,

Gt. Gable from Haystacks

and Honister Pass lies almost underneath on the right. This is the only point where the three lakes of the Buttermere valley are seen in a line.

The descent is down the top of a long, grassy ridge towards Buttermere, but there are several dangerous crags which must be avoided with care. Near the bottom, bear right to join the Honister Pass road at Gatesgarth Farm, then follow the road back to Buttermere.

Distance :—Buttermere to Red Pike and Black Beck Tarn, 8 miles. Direct descent to Buttermere, 4 miles, via Fleetwith, $6\frac{1}{2}$ miles. Time in minutes :—Ascent of Red Pike, 90; Scarth Gap Pass, 70; Haystacks, 30; Gatesgarth via Warnscale Bottom, 60; via Fleetwith, 120.

GREAT GABLE

Gt. Gable forms a grand round from Buttermere. Follow the lake-side footpath to Gatesgarth, and immediately after passing through the gate across the road near the farm, take the bridle-track which starts on the right. This winds round the foot of Warnscale Bottom, then ascends sharply up the fell side.

Towards the top, cross the beck, and follow a footpath which strikes diagonally across the side of Brandreth until it reaches the summit of the long ridge. Keep to this as it continues on to Green Gable; then follows a sharp drop into Wind Gap, after which the track becomes a rough footpath which winds in and over the huge boulders as it leads to the top of Gt. Gable.

The view is grand and extensive and includes Wastwater, Windermere, Derwentwater and Crummock lakes, and most of the principal fells.

To return follow the track back to Wind Gap. Then strike a footpath which leads off to the left, from the bottom of the gap, and goes under the crags on the north side of Gt. Gable, along the North Traverse. These are very fine rocks, and contain several noted climbs. The path then drops down to the depression between Gable and Kirk Fell.

For a short distance it follows a track called Moses Sledgate, an old smugglers' route which comes from Honister over Brandreth under the crags of Great Gable, and then down Wasdale Fell by Gavel Neese. Just before the path begins to drop towards Wasdale, leave it and make a direct line for the summit of Kirk Fell. The path is well cairned and bears left to Beckhead Tarn. Then turn left and follow a wire fence to the summit.

From the top is a good view of Scafell and the Pikes towering behind Lingmell, whilst farther west are the Screes and a splendid view of Wastwater. To the west is the Pillar, while across the Liza Valley is the High Stile range, and farther back the Robinson group. Close at hand is Gt. Gable, bounded on each side by its magnificent crags.

The descent is made in a direct line for the Bothy observed at the bottom. It is rough grass and scree, and there are several crags which must be avoided; rather steep in parts the descent requires care. Near the bottom it strikes the Black Sail Pass, and this is followed to the bottom, then take the track to the right which leads over Scarth Gap Pass back to Buttermere. Return to Buttermere village by keeping to the left of the lake and following the pleasant footpath along the lake shore underneath High Stile.

Distance, 14 miles. Time in minutes :—ascent, 180. Descent to Bothy, 120; Buttermere, 90.

SCALE FORCE—MELBREAK

This is a pleasant circular walk of Crummock Water, but the climb over Melbreak may be omitted if an easy walk with no climbing is desired.

Start from Buttermere by passing to the right of the Fish Hotel. The path strikes left and then right, following a cart track through the fields to across the river by a stone bridge. Skirting the beck, the path follows the lake shore for three quarters of a mile, bends left just beyond a small islet, crosses Scale Beck, and joins a well defined footpath coming up from the lake. This follows the course of the beck for about three-quarters of a mile, keeping to the left fork, until a fence is reached. Passing through an iron gate, the path crosses the beck by a plank, and above you are the highest falls in England, Scale Force, which drops sheer for 120 feet.

Returning down the path towards the lake, leave it just below the point where the stream is joined by another on the left. Then cross over the valley and climb up the slopes on the far side on to Melbreak. The climb up the grassy slope is steep, but short, and there appears to be no actual summit, which really consists of a long ridge providing some good views of Steeple, Pillar, Gable and Helvellyn, the lakes and the Solway.

Follow the full length of the ridge and descend slightly to the left at the far end. It is very craggy and involves scrambling down a rough scree shoot. If it should be desired to miss this, descend down the steep grassy slope on the left from about half-way along the ridge into Mosedale, then follow the bridle-track down the valley to Kirkstile.

20

A footpath goes round the foot of Crummock Water close to the water, crosses the river at the waterworks, and enters Scale Woods. Follow the narrow road along and above the lake for about a quarter-of-a-mile to the boat landing. Keep close to the lake along a footpath through the wood, and proceed along the fields by the lake shore for about a mile until the path finally joins the main road leading round Rannerdale Knott back to Buttermere.

If Melbreak is to be avoided, return from Scale Force by the beck to the lake, then continue to walk round the lake at the bottom of Melbreak. There is a good footpath all the way and no further description is necessary. It is very boggy in wet weather.

Distance:—Scale Force, 3 miles; full distance round the lake, 10 miles. Time in minutes:—Scale Force, 60; Melbreak, 50; Waterworks, 45; Buttermere Village, 75.

ROBINSON—DALE HEAD

There are still two fells in the Buttermere valley which have not been mentioned—Robinson and Dale Head. Actually they are outside the area this book intended to cover, but as they do form part of the Buttermere valley, it will be perhaps in order to refer to them.

The best way to cover these fells is to start from Stair at the Keswick end of Newlands Pass, and climb by High Snab Bank, an interesting ridge, on to Robinson. Continue across the next ridge to Dale Head, dropping down to the tarn. One may then proceed either down the pass below Eel Crags by Newlands Beck to Little Town, or if the time and energy permits, to climb up from Lobstone Bank on to Scawdel Fell and over Maiden Moor and Catbells to Swinside, which is rather a better walk than the former. Unfortunately, this walk with its wonderful views is mostly outside our area.

There is, however, quite a good round from Buttermere, starting along a path on the right-hand side of Newlands Pass (or Buttermere Hause) a short distance above Buttermere Church. A quite good track leads in a rather stiff climb up to Buttermere Moss, then carries on at an easier gradient until it nears the top to Robinson,

Buttermere Birch

when there is a sharp, short scramble to the summit. This patch was originally constructed by Earl Boethar during his fights against the Norman invaders, for he used this mountain when signalling his army.

From its stoney summit, Crummock and Loweswater can be seen below, and if one walks a short distance north, Derwentwater comes into view. Across Fleetwith Pike, the mass of Great Gable is very prominent, with the summit of Scafell Pikes directly behind. Farther west is a splendid view of the Pillar Mountain and nearer at hand Grasmoor and the Sail ridge are seen.

There is now an easy grassy drop towards Dale Head, followed by a pleasant ridge walk. The wire fence makes a good guide. If desired, a divergence can be made to the left for about a half mile on to Hindscarth, from where may be obtained a good view of Derwentwater with Skiddaw and Saddleback in the background.

Farther along the ridge one obtains glimpses of Honister Pass deep below on the right. The path then rises sharply to the summit of Dale Head, 2,473 feet, the highest point of this particular group. The view includes many of the fells previously observed from Robinson with the addition of Bowfell and Langdale Pikes. Behind these on a clear day can be seen the Yorkshire fells.

To return to Buttermere, proceed south to southeast with Dale Head Tarn—a small sheet of water almost directly below and due west of the fell summit—on your left. A wire fence is a good guide, and by keeping it on your left, it will lead down to join Honister Pass near the summit. A longer route is to drop down the rough fell side to Dale Head Tarn, although it is difficult to follow any set footpath. Just beyond the tarn, in a hollow between Scawdel Fell and High Scawdel known as Lobstone Band, several routes converge. Take the route which goes south along the side of High Scawdell, being careful not to take the more obvious track which drops to Rosthwaite. Our track descends diagonally down the side of High Scawdel, and joins the old Honister Pass road a short distance above the junction from Grange and Seatoller. Proceed up the pass to return to Buttermere.

From the top of Honister Pass, the shortest route is directly down the pass by the motor road. A more pleas-

Crummock Water

ant route is to follow the path up to the drum house, then bear right over the top of Honister Crag on to Fleetwith Pike. There is a magnificent view from here, with the three lakes of the Buttermere valley almost in line.

The descent in the direction of Buttermere lies down a sharp ridge, steep on either side, and care must be taken to keep to the path down the top of the ridge because of the crags below each side. The track is easy to follow and joins the road at the foot of Honister Pass at Gatesgarth. There is a delightful walk back to the village.

Shortly after leaving Gatesgarth, at the point where the road leaves the lake shore, a cart track commences on the left and drops to a gate. From here is a delightful shore path—which in one place passes through a tunnel in the rock—following the full length of the lake to Buttermere village.

Distance, 10 miles.   Time in minutes :—Robinson, 90 ; Hindscarth, 40 ; Dale Head, 30 ; Honister Pass, 30 ; Fleetwith Pike, 45 ; Gatesgarth, 45 ; Buttermere, 45.